ATHLETICS: TRACK EVENTS

Pelham Pictorial Sports Instruction Series

John Le Masurier and
Denis Watts MBE

ATHLETICS:
TRACK EVENTS

Pelham Books

First published in Great Britain by
PELHAM BOOKS LTD
52 Bedford Square
London WC1B 3EF
1977

ISBN 0 7207 0970 9

Filmset and printed in Great Britain by
BAS Printers Limited, Wallop, Hampshire

Contents

Picture credits

Photographs
Tissot von Patot—sprint start, middle-distance running and steeplechase
    sequence shots.
Toni Nett—baton-passing sequence.
All other photographs are by Mervyn Rees, FRPS

Line drawings
Figures 54 and 55 are reproduced by kind permission of the Amateur
Athletic Association from the *AAA Handbook.*

Introduction

This book has been written for young athletes interested in track events. The authors have attempted to cover only the basic fundamentals of each event, those simple skills and basic instructions which will enable novices to improve and progress to a higher level of performance in their chosen event or events.

The emphasis is on 'how to do it' but the text also includes hints on conditioning for endurance events. Once newcomers to the sport have proved to themselves that they have certain skills, the interest will be there to train hard and develop slowly all the physical characteristics that go to make a champion. It is worth remembering, however, that accomplished performers in athletics, or any sport for that matter, do not appear overnight. The best athletes have practised seriously and sensibly to develop the skills with which they have been endowed.

The authors hope that this book will encourage many girls and boys of all ages to enjoy athletics and to find success and satisfaction from taking part in the world's oldest sport.

The book is divided into five chapters: sprinting, relays, hurdles, middle-distance running and steeplechase. Every chapter is illustrated with photographic sequences showing both young athletes learning the skills of each event and accomplished performers in action.

CHAPTER ONE

Sprinting

The word 'sprinting' means 'running at full speed' and is the basic feature of all athletic events. Every young athlete should practise running fast because speed is vital in so many sports. Even the distance runner must remember to train his speed as well as his stamina. In his run to the finishing line he may be outsprinted by the clever athlete who has learned to change his action from an easy, relaxed style, to a powerful, driving sprint action.

Every child is born with a certain quota of natural speed. Some undoubtedly are much more gifted in this respect than others. However small the quota of natural ability one has, there are certainly many ways in which it is possible to improve the ability to run fast.

1. The starter is in command. It is his job to ensure that the start is a fair one and that all the athletes are motionless when the gun fires.

Athletics: Track Events

It is essential to sprint with a fluent, balanced action which reflects perfect synchronisation between the arms and the legs. For adults, all races up to 400 metres are considered to be sprints. For youngsters, however, it is better to class the 400 metres as one of the middle distances.

The start

The start of all races is crucial and is in the hands of the starter (Fig. 1). When he gives the words of command 'On your marks!', the athletes walk from behind an assembly line to their starting positions. His next command is 'Set!', then when all the runners are ready and perfectly still he fires the gun. If any athlete moves before the gun is fired, he will be warned and if this happens again he will probably be disqualified. This whole procedure calls for a great deal of concentration and practice. The time between the command 'Set!' and the firing of the gun is normally about 2 to 3 seconds, but this depends on how long it takes for the athletes to be steady.

The standing start

There are two starting positions an athlete may adopt—the standing start and the crouch start—but initially, and especially for younger runners, it is a good plan to learn an effective standing start.

On the command 'On your marks!' the athlete adopts the position shown in Fig. 2. The front foot is placed as close to the starting line as possible with a spread of about fourteen inches between the feet. The toes of both feet point directly forward. The hands are placed on the leading knee in a relaxed and comfortable position.

2. 'On your marks!'. In the standing start the leading foot can be placed as close to the start line as possible. The athlete relaxes with the hands on the thigh.

10

On the command 'Set!', the arms take up a position from which they can move immediately into a sprinting action, and at the same time the shoulders and trunk move down and forward (Fig. 3). The problem here, however, is that it is difficult to hold this position and still remain rock steady because the body weight is so far forward. It is important to remember that the back leg moves first to take up the running.

3. 'Set!'. The shoulders have moved forward and down. The right arm has moved forward and the left arm back so that when the gun fires they can synchronise with the legs.

The crouch start

The aim of an effective starting position is to produce immediate and powerful acceleration when the gun fires. In the crouch start the sprinter's main body mass is centred in the head and trunk. This mass must be driven forward by the action of the legs and arms. In the same way that a car's engine is revved up and is started in low gear, the athlete must produce a fast explosive action to accelerate the body mass.

The essential features of the starting position are shown in Figs. 4, 5 and 6 and can be described as follows:
1. Starting blocks are set up in the centre of the lane, pointing straight down the track. The blocks are placed so that the athlete's leading foot is about sixteen inches behind the starting line with the front block angled at 55°–60°. The rear block is placed twelve to fourteen inches further back with a more vertical block angle.

4. The 'on your marks' position for the crouch start.

5. Crouch start—front view. Note how the hands are placed with the weight supported on the tips of the fingers and thumb.

2. The hands are placed behind the starting line with fingers turned outward and thumbs inward. The arms are shoulder width apart and the head looks down, with neck muscles relaxed. The body weight is supported on the tips of the fingers and thumbs.

6. The 'set' position for the crouch start.

3. The all-essential 'set' position in Fig. 6 shows how the seat has been raised and the legs have opened out to an angle of 90° at the front knee, which is the most efficient angle for driving against the block. The body weight is poised ahead of the legs and the shoulders have moved immediately above the starting line. A deep breath is taken and held on the command 'Set!'. This fixes the chest and helps the athlete to concentrate on the start.

14

The gun

When the gun fires there must be an immediate reaction which results in a vigorous thrust by both feet against the blocks. At the same time the arms drive in a counterbalancing action (Fig. 7). The speed of the legs and arms, combined with concentrated thrust against the blocks, helps to produce a fast start. The athlete must practise this, directing all his or her energy into the line of running.

The first strides of a sprint race will be short, gradually lengthening as the trunk rises to an upright position, which it should assume after nine or ten strides. The head is important here. It must be kept in alignment with the shoulders and must not be forced back, as this will destroy the low carriage of the trunk so essential during the acceleration phase.

Figures 8–15 show the complete starting action.

Leg action

Speed over the ground is produced by balancing stride length with leg speed. Both are equally important and both must be practised. Stride length will be improved through greater joint mobility, flexibility and muscular strength. Mobility in the hip region is most important, as this largely determines whether the sprinter is able to run with the high knee action so critical to good performance. Knees and feet must be directed straight down the track.

Arm action

As has already been mentioned, the arms help the getaway action from the blocks—they help leg speed by themselves initiating a fast tempo. They

7. The gun has fired! Speed of legs and arms combine with concentrated thrust against the starting blocks. The trunk is low during this vital period of acceleration.

have another function which is to work in perfect synchronisation with the legs, counterbalancing any twisting which

15

8

9

12

13

8–15. The complete action of starting, perfectly demonstrated by Britain's Andrea Lynch, Olympic 100 metres finalist, and one of the world's fastest starters.

would otherwise result from powerful leg drives. Finally, the arms help to keep the legs moving when fatigue sets in. Concentration must be focused on driving the elbows back and producing a big range of swing.

Tension
All young athletes are faced with the problem of tension, which can seriously

10

11

14

15

hamper their running style. This shows itself particularly in the face, neck and shoulder muscles. To overcome this athletes should practise running at varying speeds trying to retain a natural carriage of the head and shoulders. It is difficult to channel effort into the arms and legs and at the same time retain relaxation in the rest of the body, particularly when the muscles are tired,

but it can be achieved with practice.

Drills

The modern sprinter must incorporate a number of essential drill practices in his training. Remember that the ultimate aim is to improve SPEED, which is determined by an improvement in stride length and leg speed. To be of value drills must be related to an improvement in these

17

factors. Here are seven examples which can be used as a complete training session, with each drill repeated two or three times:

1. Driving practice for stride length. The athlete uses a standing start and at every stride concentrates on straightening the legs behind the hips in the driving action, at the same time working on a high thigh lift in front. (20–30 metres)

2. Running fast for relaxation. Emphasise relaxed face, neck and shoulder muscles. (50 metres)

3. Running (almost on the spot) with high knee raising (Fig. 16). Emphasise an upright carriage of the body and vigorous use of the arms. (10 with each leg)

4. Step running (Fig. 17). This is an excellent drill which can be varied according to requirements. It encourages knee lift, leg and ankle extension and a powerful arm action. (e.g. 4 × 20 steps, 2 steps at a time)

5. 'Tripplings'. This is a leg speed exercise in which the feet and arms are moved as fast as possible. The feet should hardly leave the ground. (20 metres)

6. Running for style. Concentrate on keeping the hips high and the shoulders steady. Work the arms through a full range, particularly driving the elbows backwards in perfect synchronisation with the legs. (30–40 metres)

7. Finishing drill. Practise running at full speed through a finishing line. Aim to run at least 10 metres beyond the line before slowing down. Do not look sideways. (40 metres)

16. *Running, almost on the spot, with high knee raising.*

17. Step running—an excellent conditioner for the sprinter.

CHAPTER TWO

Relay Racing

Relay races are usually the last events in the Sports Day programme. By their very nature these races produce a climax of excitement. There is always the possibility of a well-drilled group of average sprinters passing the baton really well and defeating a more highly fancied team of faster runners. Also, there is always the chance of a dropped baton.

The baton
The baton is a hollow tube made usually of metal but sometimes of wood. It should measure between 28 and 30 cm in length. The rules recommend that it be coloured so as to be easily visible during a race. If the baton is dropped, it must be recovered by the athlete who dropped it.

Take-over zones
The most usual relay race is the 4 × 100 metres. For this event there are three 20 metre take-over zones (or 'boxes') marked on the track. These are sited at 100-, 200- and 300-metre marks. Before each 'box' there is also marked an extra 10-metre area which is known as the acceleration zone. The outgoing runner is allowed to start his run in this area, but the actual passing of the baton must take place within the 20-metre take-over zone. It is best to pass the baton with at least a 5-metre margin of safety from the far end of the 'box'. To pass outside the 'box' will result in disqualification.

The passing of the baton is completed at the moment it is in the hand of the receiving runner. The judge looks at the position of the baton in relation to the take-over zone, not at the position of the individual runners at the moment of exchange.

Baton passing
The very essence of efficient relay racing is good team work and slick baton passing. The aim is for the runners to pass the baton with confidence, blending the speed of the incoming runner with that of the outgoing partner without any hesitation.

It is normal for the first runner to carry the baton in the right hand (Fig. 18). On a normal track the take-over zone is at the end of the first bend, and here the No. 2 runner receives the baton in his left hand. He then runs the length of the back straight before passing to No. 3, who receives the baton in his right hand. No. 3 then runs the second bend and

18. The first runner carries the baton in the right hand, firmly holding it at one end. It is a matter of personal preference as to which fingers are used to grasp it as long as it is held safely.

passes to the left hand of No. 4, who is known as the 'anchor man'.

This method of passing, using right hand to left hand to right hand to left hand, is known as the 'alternate' method. When carried out efficiently it is fast and effective because at no stage do the athletes have to change the baton from one hand to the other. However, some coaches and teachers of younger athletes prefer to have all their runners receiving

in one hand and then passing the baton to their other hand. In this method the first runner starts with the baton in the left hand and all the other team members receive in the right hand and immediately switch the baton to the left hand.

Whichever method the team is employing, the actual technique of passing is the same. The 'upsweep pass', as it is known, is made by the incoming runner sweeping the baton upward into the V shape made by the forefinger and thumb of the outgoing runner's hand (see Fig. 19). This is a very natural movement which requires very little deviation from the sprinter's normal arm action.

Check marks
In order to blend the speed of the outgoing runner with that of the incoming partner, the receiver must time his start precisely to the moment when his partner crosses a clearly visible pre-determined check mark. This must be measured back from the receiver's starting point. The distance is usually measured in heel-to-toe foot lengths and will probably be about eighteen to twenty foot lengths. The precise distance of the check mark from the outgoing

19. *The pass is made with an upsweeping action into the V made by the receiver's forefinger and thumb. The baton is passed well forward into the receiver's hand.*

runner's starting point is critical and can only be finalised as a result of much practice.

Teamwork

The outgoing runner must adopt an efficient standing start. He must position himself so that he can turn his shoulders to look back towards his incoming partner. At the moment the incoming sprinter reaches the check mark, the receiver must turn his head and shoulders to the front and start sprinting.

20. The centre line of the take-over zone has been crossed and the incoming runner is ready to call 'Hand!'. Note the full-blooded driving action of the outgoing runner.

21. In this second exchange the pass is being made at full speed from left hand to right hand. Note how the outgoing runner is looking straight ahead and is confident of receiving the baton at speed.

When the incoming runner feels that he is almost within striking distance, he must call 'Hand!' and thrust the baton up into his partner's hand. The receiver must keep his hand perfectly steady and must not look back at any time. The exchange is non-visual. See Figs. 20 and 21.

The incoming runner must appreciate that the outgoing runner is building up acceleration at every stride, so he cannot afford to ease up at any stage until after the baton has been passed. He must pass as much of the baton as he can into his

23

25

24

29

28

22–29. This sequence shows the first change of an Olympic relay race with the baton being passed from right hand to left. The incoming and outgoing speeds have blended perfectly so that efficient baton passing has been achieved.

partner's hand, and then remain in his lane until all the incoming runners from the other teams have passed.

The outgoing runner must learn to start at the precise moment that the check mark is reached. More passes are muffed because the outgoing runner has failed in this respect than for any other reason. The outgoing runner must also learn to present a steady hand. If one considers

23

22

27

26

the receiving hand to be a target which must be hit by the passer, it will be understood why it must be steady. Furthermore, if the incoming runner fails to make contact at the first attempt it is imperative for the receiver to keep his hand steady and to avoid the great tendency to start feeling for the baton, as this only makes it more difficult for the passer. Study the sequence pictures,

Figs. 22–29.

Practices

The importance of baton-passing practice cannot be over-emphasised. The skill of passing and receiving the baton must be performed as frequently as possible. Every opportunity to practise should be taken; even the warm-up period for a training session can be used.

For example, four athletes can jog round the track in single file constantly passing the baton forwards and backwards to one another.

Another practice which is very valuable requires an odd number of runners. Five works very well. The runners line up 25 to 30 metres apart with the first runner (at the rear of the line) carrying the baton in the right hand. As he runs, No. 2 moves away and waits for No. 1's call to put his left hand back, and so on until No. 5 receives the baton, when the whole procedure is repeated in reverse order.

Naturally, there must also be practices at full speed in which the team members establish and record check-mark distances. Experience shows that there is a good tie-up between check marks worked out in training, where the incoming runner covers 50 metres, and the marks required for a full-distance race.

Frequent practice will help to breed confidence and understanding, so important in the training of a competent relay squad. The time spent in perfecting passes will bring rich rewards in matches against other teams who have faster individual runners, but who have not practised to perfection.

CHAPTER THREE

Hurdling

To hurdle really well requires sprinting ability combined with fluent hurdling style.

Because the hurdles are placed at pre-set distances, it is necessary for the athlete to adopt a definite number of strides from the start to the first hurdle, and to take a set number of strides between the hurdles. In hurdle races from 70 to 100 metres it is usual to use either seven or eight strides in covering the approach to the first hurdle, and a stride pattern of three strides between the hurdles.

	Distance (m)	No. of hurdles	Hurdle height (cm)	Approach distance (m)	Between (m)	Run in (m)
Under 13 years						
Boys and girls	70	8	68	11	7	10
Under 14 years						
Girls	70	8	76	11	7	10
Boys	75	8	76	11.5	7.5	11
Under 15 years						
Girls	75	8	76	11.5	7.5	11
Boys	80	8	84	12	8	12
Under 17 years						
Girls	80	8	76	12	8	12
Boys	100	10	92	13	8.5	10.5

Athletics: Track Events

The adoption of these stride patterns is not always simple, because youngsters come in all shapes and sizes within the same age-group. Whilst a three-stride pattern between hurdles may be easy for the long-legged youngster, it may be a bit of a stretch for some of his shorter opponents. However, the shorter athlete may be gifted with more basic speed, which will help to compensate for his lack of inches. It is variables such as these which make hurdling events so attractive to boys and girls of all ages.

The main races for young hurdlers are given on page 27.

Technique

The essence of good hurdling is to cross the barriers at speed with as little break in natural sprint rhythm as possible. From the outset it must be clearly understood that hurdlers do not jump their obstacles, but drive across them at full speed (Fig. 30). In order to accomplish the essential fluency of action, the athlete must depart as little as possible from his normal running action.

30. Attacking the first hurdle. The athlete on the near side shows excellent form in driving across the barrier.

The start

The start is similar to that used by the sprinter except that:

(a) the hurdler must be ready to cross his first hurdle after eight strides, therefore rising to his normal running action a shade sooner, and
(b) his starting action must bring him to a precise point on the track so that he can take off accurately to clear the first obstacle. This distance will vary from one athlete to another but will be something in excess of 190 cm from the hurdle.

The start and the approach run to the first hurdle call for much practice. In a race it is a great advantage to be leading at the first hurdle.

Leading leg

The leg which lifts across the hurdle is known as the leading leg; the other is known as the trailing leg. It is the leading leg which largely dictates the effectiveness of the clearance. In order to move really fast this leg must be flexed at the knee and ankle and must be lifted directly forward in the line of running. As the leading thigh rises so the leg will hinge out from the knee, the aim being to move the leading leg up and across the barrier and down onto the track as quickly as possible.

At take-off it is essential to thrust the opposite arm and shoulder forward and, at the same time, to dip the chest across the leading thigh. By emphasising these actions the shoulders are kept square to the front (Fig. 31).

The trailing leg

The take-off power for clearance is produced by the leg which becomes the

31. Crossing the hurdle. The leading leg is moving down in the line of running whilst the trailing leg makes room for the hurdle rail by sweeping laterally. This allows the athlete to keep low and to spend as little time in the air as possible.

trailing leg. After take-off the heel folds in close to the buttock and the folded leg is swept round laterally over the hurdle rail (Fig. 31). This allows the athlete to keep low. It must constantly be borne in mind that any hesitancy over the hurdles has a slowing effect; speed must be underlined all the time.

After the trailing leg crosses the hurdle rail the rotary sweep of the thigh must continue until the knee is pulled through high to the centre line of the body. This action ensures a strong follow-up stride on landing. The trunk lean which started at take-off must be maintained until clearance is completed.

Exercises for the development of the trailing leg are given at the end of this chapter (see Figs. 39–41).

Between hurdles
Running from one hurdle to the next requires great balance and concentration. The three-stride action must eat up the ground so that the hurdler is ready to take off accurately for the next hurdle and is completely in control. It is important for hurdlers to skim low over the hurdles in order to avoid hesitancy, but it is also important to remember that the hips must be held high at all times.

As the hurdler approaches his obstacle he must try to look down on it rather than to think of it as an obstacle which he must rise up to. He must keep high on the balls of his feet in take-off, in landing and in running between the hurdles.

Suppleness and mobility
It is impossible for an athlete who is stiff in the joints and lacking in mobility to become a good hurdler. All aspiring hurdlers must work daily to improve their suppleness. This applies particularly to the hip region where stiffness prevents the fluent action of the legs, essential to efficient hurdle crossing.

The following exercises, if performed regularly, will gradually improve the range of movement, mobility of joint and suppleness of muscle:

1. Ground Hurdling
The athlete should adopt the starting position shown in Fig. 32 then bend forward from as low down the trunk as possible, at the same time reaching forward with the right shoulder and arm (Fig. 33).

2. Side-lungeing
This exercise, shown in Figs. 34–35, helps to mobilise the hips, knees and ankles. The athlete should move freely from left to right, pressing down easily over the flexed legs.

3. Leg swinging
Figures 36–37 illustrate another good exercise for improving hip mobility. The athlete grasps a convenient rail and then swings the leg loosely from side to side, allowing the standing foot to turn with the swing. Gradually the range of swing can be increased until it reaches the height shown in Fig. 37.

32–33. (right) Ground-hurdling exercise.

34–35. (left) Side-lungeing exercise.

36–37. (below) Leg-swinging exercise to mobilise the hips.

38. Leg-swinging exercise to improve the action of the leading leg.

Figure 38 shows a leg-swinging exercise to improve the action of the leading leg. The athlete grasps the bar side-on and swings the leg forward and backward.

39–41 (below and right) An exercise to develop the correct action of the trailing leg.

4. *Trailing-leg exercise*

For this exercise a hurdle should be placed in front of a convenient rail as shown in Fig. 39. The athlete grasps the bar and stands at one end of the hurdle. The trailing leg is pulled through and over the hurdle in a lateral sweep with the knee high and the foot pulled well in to the seat (Fig. 40). It is important to continue the sweep so that the knee finishes high in front (Fig. 41). The leg is then allowed to drop back to the starting point (Fig. 39) and the action repeated.

The speed at which this exercise is performed should gradually increase as the movement is mastered. Emphasis should be placed on *lifting* the thigh over the hurdle.

CHAPTER FOUR

The Middle Distances

The middle distances for boys and girls consist of the 800 m and 1500 m events, however for very young runners the 400 m may also be classed as a middle-distance event. Although there is little point in attempting to break down a runner's individual style, much can be done at an early age to improve technique and, therefore, improve the athlete's speed and ability to accelerate. The middle-distance runner should refer to the opening paragraphs of the chapter on sprinting and the running drills on page 17.

Technique (see Figs. 42–50)
In sprinting, the runner should move the arms quickly in an attempt to dictate, to some extent, the speed of the legs. In middle-distance running, the arms are used to balance the leg action and should move from the shoulders with a natural easy swing slightly across the body to the middle line of the trunk.

The leg action is modified to that of sprinting. The cadence is not so rapid and the knee lift not so exaggerated, but at the same time sufficient stride length

42. David McMeekin (GB, 800 m in 1.46.8) illustrates the typical form of a first-class 800 m runner.

must be maintained. The ball of the foot should land fractionally before the heel (see Fig. 42) and then, during the supporting phase of the cycle of leg movement, the heel of the foot will contact the ground. This provides a momentary rest for the calf muscles as the body moves over the supporting leg bent at the knee (Figs. 44 and 45). This action will be more apparent in the 800 m runner than in an athlete concentrating more on 5000 m and 10,000 m distances.

Although, during training sessions, overstriding can at times be a beneficial exercise, if the novice attempts this in competition it will prove extremely fatiguing and the results will be disastrous. The inexperienced runner can win races in spite of understriding but seldom, if ever, by overstriding.

The forward lean of the body will not be as great in middle-distance running as in sprinting. The amount of lean depends on other factors besides the force exerted against the ground by the legs and, therefore, it is better for the athlete to concentrate on performing the movements of the limbs correctly and, in time, the body lean will adjust itself to the physical characteristics of the athlete and natural method of running.

However, the most important factor in middle-distance and long-distance running is the correct conditioning of the athlete for the distance over which he or she will race. The young athlete will do well to concentrate on going for steady runs and participating in cross-country training and competition. In this way the beginner will become conditioned to the harder, more specific work which must follow later on.

Tactics

Tactics and pace judgement go hand in hand: sound tactics will enable the runner to make the best use of pace judgement. Tactical sense will develop as the athlete gains more experience and, to this end, attempts should be made to learn from every race. It is advisable to have a coach or knowledgeable friend watching all the early races to help in analysing mistakes after the race.

The start

The athlete should attempt to get into a good position as early as possible in the race. To this end the first 200 m is generally run at a fast pace then the runners settle down to a regular pace for the middle part of the race. If a runner draws an outside position at the start, it is rarely a good thing to attempt to take the lead. To do this, the runner would have to exert tremendous effort, running a greater distance at a faster speed than his counterparts placed in the inside positions. In such a situation it is better to work through the field into a suitable position from behind and let the more favourably placed runners fight it out for the leading positions. Fig. 51 shows the start of a major race with a field of world-class runners; note carefully the jostling taking place.

It is recommended that a shorter stride and a higher arm action be employed in the early, hurly-burly jockeying for position. In the 800 m, where the first part of the race is run in lanes, the runner must have a good knowledge of pace if he is to come out of the stagger in a good position. Starting practice, running the appropriate distance in the correct time, will pay dividends when the runner

43

44

47

48

38   *43–50. David Bedford, British world-record beater (10,000 m in 27.47.0), showing superb running technique in a distance event.*

45

46

49

50

51. The start of the Emsley Carr Mile, 1975. Note the bumping and jostling taking place.

has to compete against good opposition.

The middle of the race
Assuming the competitors are of roughly the same ability, it is better tactically to run in either second or third position during this part of the race. Most runners find it less tiring to follow than to lead and lying in second or third position a runner can, when necessary, take the lead. Running just off the shoulder of the leader is very often a good tactical position because it is possible to dictate, to some extent, how the race is to be run. If there is a challenge from behind, it can easily be fought off; the athlete may take the lead at any time and there is no likelihood of being boxed in.

Passing
All passing must be done briskly, accelerating rapidly from behind and the effort continuing for several metres beyond the opposition. If this passing movement is made sluggishly, without attack, the opponent will be encouraged to fight back; in this case it becomes a tussle which neither runner can afford. One should not pass on a bend unless it is absolutely necessary.

The finish
The best tactics here depend on the speed and condition of the individual at the end of the race. Sometimes it is a good thing to put in a long sustained finishing burst in order to catch the

opposition by surprise. The runner should be prepared to start the finishing effort any time after entering the back straight. At all costs, once the final burst has been commenced there must be no weakening or change of mind. If the home straight is a long one, then it may be best to be off the leader's shoulder as

52. Brendan Foster, 10,000 m bronze medallist in the 1976 Olympics, takes the lead and sets the pace in this distance event.

he comes off the final bend. In this case the acceleration should be made rapidly from behind at the entry to the home straight. The runner who has the courage to take the initiative firmly at this point is very often the winner.

Training methods

A runner may prepare for competition in many ways but, in the end, the choice will depend upon the facilities at his disposal, the time available for training and, to some extent, his own personal preference for one type of work over another. This does not mean that young runners should train just as they please but rather, where there are several methods of gaining the same end, they should select the mixture of the available methods which give them most enjoyment and personal satisfaction. For instance, many first-class senior runners prefer to do most of their work away from the track by doing forms of fartlek—fast and slow work through woods and countryside—rather than the more regimented forms of interval running on the track. The 800/1500 m runners will be doing more work which is anaerobic in nature and the long distance runners more aerobic training.

In aerobic work the runner's oxygen uptake keeps pace with the oxygen requirements of the race or training session. This means long, steady-paced running and for a boy running 800 m this will mean runs of 3 to 6 miles, and 5 to 10 miles for the 1500 m runner. This type of work improves oxygen uptake and the present world status of our distance runners is due, in the main, to the very big mileages our top athletes carry out in training. Anaerobic training is where the athlete runs at fast speeds with short recoveries to ensure that his oxygen requirement will exceed his oxygen uptake. In simple language, he gets out of breath quickly and continues to work with the products of fatigue in the body. This work simulates the effects of running 800/1500 m where runners go into high oxygen debt. The types of training that produce these effects are: interval running, repetition running, speed-endurance running, fartlek and time trials.

There is no point in describing these types of training in detail for the beginner because the schedule should not include many track sessions of a hard or exacting nature. The athlete should rather be preparing with steady runs, enjoyable fartlek and only the occasional track session against a watch. A proportion of track work should include pace-judgement work so the runner learns to run at the correct pace in order to complete the distance in the best possible time. For example: Assuming the track to be 400 m, a young athlete who is aiming to run the 1500 m in 4 min 22·5 secs can have the track divided into four quarters with a flag placed at every 100 m. In order to achieve his goal he will need to lap this distance in 70 secs, so that the first flag should be passed in 17·5 secs, the second flag in 35 secs, the third flag in 52·5 secs and the last in 70 secs. The coach should blow a whistle at every elapsed time and the athlete will know whether to speed up or slow the pace in order to finish the lap in the correct time. After a period of rest, the exercise can be repeated and in this way the runner will develop a knowledge of even-pace running.

53. Harness running—a useful training technique.

Harness Running

Figure 53 shows how technique and strength may be improved with the use of a harness fitted round the athlete's waist. The coach controls the exercise by offering resistance as the runner drives forward. In this way the movements of the arms and legs are exaggerated and good technique is encouraged. The coach must offer only enough resistance to slow the athlete down, making him increase both the force and range of his limb movements in order to move forward. Harness work may be carried out during the winter and early spring as an adjunct to normal training sessions.

43

CHAPTER FIVE

Steeplechase

The best young steeplechasers generally emerge from runners who combine fast times on the track over distances from 1500 m upwards with a natural enthusiasm for cross-country running. They also, as a rule, are rangy, rugged boys who can withstand hard knocks and enjoy hard work. The young athlete who is a natural hurdler has a big advantage over the normal track specialist because much time has to be spent mastering the skill of hurdling and water jumping. In this respect one should refer to the chapter on hurdling and, in particular, the exercises for mobility (pages 30–35).

As a rough guide, the young runner should think in terms of adding 18 secs to his best time for 1500 m over a flat distance and set himself this target in competition. So a runner who has managed 4 mins for 1500 m flat would hope to achieve 4 mins 18 secs for 1500 m steeplechase. This will, of course, largely depend on his ability to clear the barriers and to master his strides and approach to each obstacle. The differentials for the world's best 3000 m steeplechasers and their times over the flat 3000 m vary from approximately 20 to 30 secs. The faster time the runner has over the flat distance the greater his chance of becoming a champion steeplechaser. It was this that enabled David Bedford (GB), with very little experience of steeplechasing, to run a 3000 m steeplechase in 8 mins 28·6 secs. His best time for 3000 m flat was 7 mins 46·2 secs which gave him a big differential of 42.4 secs. With better technique over the barriers and a differential of 30 secs his time might in theory have been 8 mins 16·2 secs.

Steeplechase layouts
The standard distances are as follows:

Senior: 3000 m (1 mile, 1520 yd, 2 ft 8 in) 28 hurdles and 7 water jumps.
Junior: 2000 m (1 mile, 427 yd, 9 in) 18 hurdles and 5 water jumps. See Fig. 54.
Youths: 1500 m (1640 yd, 1 ft, 4 in) 13 hurdles and 3 water jumps. See Fig. 55.

Water-jump clearance
The ability to make a technically sound and, therefore, economical clearance of the water jump can make a tremendous difference to the entire race. If the water jump is negotiated badly, fatigue can

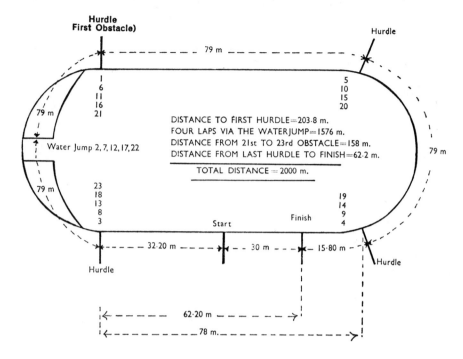

54. *Example track layout for junior steeplechase, 2000 m. (Lap length = 394 m.)*

55. *Example track layout for youth steeplechase, 1500 m. (Lap length = 394 m.)*

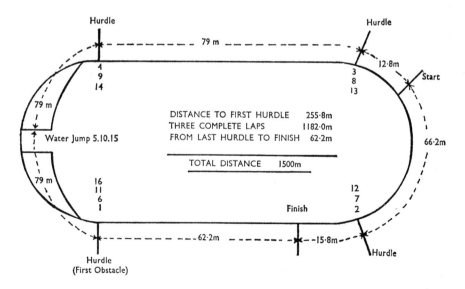

make itself felt early on in the race. The effort of picking up the speed of the race again after falling short and stumbling out of the water can cause the runner to pay a heavy price in terms of energy. However, it is not enough just to learn an easy, economical technique over the jumps; the athlete must have sufficient agility and strength to clear the barrier and water as he wishes. He must also be aware of what is going on around him; crowding and jostling at the barriers is commonplace. There is a very real danger of the athlete stumbling or falling if he allows himself to be manoeuvred into an awkward position when approaching the barriers and, in particular, the water jump.

Initially, for young novice steeplechasers, a steeplechase hurdle can be used for practising water-jump technique (see Figs. 56–58). Once this is mastered the progression to the water jump itself is a comparatively safe and easy task.

56–58. Learning to clear the water jump.
Above, rising to the hurdle, using the arms to assist with take-off.

57. *Crossing the hurdle. Having landed on top of the rail with the ball of the foot, the athlete crouches and rotates rapidly about the fulcrum of the foot to bring over the trailing leg.*

58. *Running off the hurdle. The split between the legs maintains the running action. The driving foot should be kept against the rail for as long as possible.*

The point of take-off should be $4\frac{1}{2}$–5 ft (136–152 cm) from the hurdle, depending largely on the athlete's speed of approach. As he nears the water jump, his speed should be increased slightly in order to allow him to attack the hurdle and obtain a fast economical clearance.

The beginner should practise with a check mark placed some distance back from the hurdle. This mark should be struck with the foot the athlete wishes to put on the rail and should be calculated to give him a seven-stride rhythm, the eighth stride landing on top of the rail. As a guide, the check mark should be placed some 15-16 yd (13·5–14·5 m) away from the hurdle, but measurement by heel-to-toe foot lengths will be found the easiest and most convenient method for the steeplechaser. It is not always possible or practical to place a check mark on modern synthetic track surfaces in competition, but the confidence gained by using an even-stride approach in training will stand the athlete in good stead.

As a general rule, it is better to place the take-off foot for hurdling on the rail of the water-jump hurdle. In other words, it is better to use the stronger leg to push off from the rail. However, there are exceptions to this rule and, in any case, the athlete should ensure that his weight-training programme incorporates exercises to make him strong in both legs.

Figures 59–70 illustrate the correct technique for approach, take-off, clearance and landing at a water jump. A study of this sequence and the following simple instructions will help the young steeplechaser to master the technique of water jumping:

1. The ball of the foot should be placed on the rail (Fig. 62). Good steeplechase shoes have needle spikes placed on the instep in order to obtain an immediate purchase on the wooden rail. Immediately the rail of the hurdle becomes wet and slippery, flat shoes become dangerous because they can slip and cause the athlete to fall. Therefore, spiked shoes should always be worn when going over water jumps.
2. The body should be lowered so the jumper can pivot over the foot which is placed on the rail (Fig. 63).
3. From this crouched position on top of the rail the jumper should push off. The thigh of the leading leg should reach out with the knee bent and the foot underneath the knee.
4. The driving leg should be kept pushing against the rail for as long as possible because this leads to a good running action off the hurdle and out of the water. In effect, the instruction to the athlete should be to keep the foot against the rail for as long as he can (Fig. 64).

59–70. Anders Garderud (Sw) demonstrates excellent water-jump technique during the 3000 m steeplechase final in the European Championships in Rome, 1960.

59

60

61

62

63

64

67

68

65

66

69

70

5. The trailing leg should be brought through high in order to avoid any tendency to stumble and to assist with keeping the running action going on landing (Figs. 66–68).

6. It is preferable to land near to the edge of the water and, therefore, to step out of the water on the first stride. In theory this means that the runner only gets one foot wet during the race. However, through lack of strength, endurance and agility he may find it better to drop short and run out as best he can (Figs. 68–70).

Hurdling

Although the steeplechaser does not require the polished technique of the 400 m hurdler, he should nevertheless attempt to model his style on these lines. He must develop an economical action over the hurdles for several reasons. Bad clearances use up energy which the runner will require during the later stages of the race, and also result in poor landings with the consequent effort to pick up speed again on the far side of the hurdle. A competitor cannot afford to make a mistake because the hurdles are big and heavy and can cause injury if they are struck. Good hurdling means less time is wasted in clearing the barriers and also that the athlete is less likely to run into trouble during the race.

Take-off

1. The take-off spot depends, in the main, upon the speed with which the runner approaches the hurdle. At the beginning of the race, when the athlete is fresh, it might be as far away as 6 ft (182 cm), but in the later stages, when he is tiring, it could be in as close as 5 ft

6 in. (167 cm).

2. It is recommended that the athlete keeps as near as possible to an even pace as this helps to consolidate the take-off spot. There is a slight increase in speed though as he approaches each hurdle, especially in the early part of the race; this helps in obtaining a good clearance. However, as he begins to tire towards the end of the race, he may start slowing down at each obstacle. This is often due to the fact that he is too tired to pick the leading leg up fast and has to slow down to adjust the take-off spot and get the timing right.

3. During training, the athlete must learn to judge the hurdles by doing repetition runs over one, two and three laps at racing speed with five hurdles placed at correct intervals on the track. He must be careful not to lose concentration and keep his eyes fixed firmly on the position of the next obstacle as he approaches it. Shortening the stride or stuttering before hurdles is bad; the stride must be kept going at all costs.

Crossing the hurdle (see Figs. 72–83)

1. The athlete should study the form of the 400 m hurdler and modify the technique to suit the speed of the race.

2. He should attempt to clear the hurdles without any wasted effort but will be taking them a little higher than the 400 m man because of the safety factor. (Figs. 75–77.)

3. The leading leg should be brought up fast and at right angles to the hurdle. As in normal hurdling the foot should stay underneath the knee until the knee has reached its highest point. In other words, the knee is bent as the leg rises to the hurdle; in no circumstances should the

71. T. Kantanen (Fin) leading John Bicourt (GB) over the water jump in a major
steeplechase event.

72

73

76

77

72–83. Hurdle clearance superbly executed by Anders Garderud (Sw) competing in a heat of the 3000 m steeplechase in Rome, 1974.

74

75

78

79

80

81

82

83

leg be lifted either straight or semi-straight. (Figs. 73 and 74.)

4. The leading arm must go out and down as the athlete rises to the hurdle and this, plus body-dip, will keep the shoulders square to the front. (Figs. 75–78.)

5. As the runner comes off the hurdle, he should pull the trailing leg through late but fast, in order to maintain an uninterrupted running action as he comes to the ground. (Figs. 78–83.)

84. Cross-country running is a useful and enjoyable method of training for steeplechase events. This photograph shows the start of a major boys' cross-country race.

Athletics: Track Events

Training

In the early days of a steeplechaser's career he should do a considerable amount of interval hurdling at varying distances. Sessions with five hurdles in position on a one-lap circuit should take place on two or even three days per week. In this way he becomes familiar with the pattern of the race and thus learns to take each hurdle smoothly even when he is tired, with senses dulled with fatigue. In time this can be increased to two laps, i.e. 800 m with five hurdles in each lap.

He should build up the race step by step, occasionally doing a number of laps in his racing target time. The number of laps should be increased as his strength and fitness improve. In this way he achieves a degree of confidence which allows him to go into competition with an aggressive determination to win. Fartlek, cross-country running, fell running and mountain climbs can all play an important part in building up the necessary degree of physical and mental fitness for this strenuous, challenging event.

Appendix

Standard Tables

The English Schools Athletic Association publishes the following standard tables of performance which relate to various age groups.

District Standard, marked D in the tables, corresponds to a good standard of performance by an athlete competing at a District Championship Meeting.

School Standard, marked S, corresponds to a good standard of performance by an athlete competing at a School Championship Meeting.

Boys under 13 years		D	S
		secs.	secs.
80 metres		11.6	12.2
100 metres		13.8	14.2
200 metres		29.3	30.3
400 metres		65.5	68.4
Hurdles	70 metres at 68 cm	13.0	13.3
	75 metres at 68 cm	14.0	14.8
Relay	4 × 100 m	57.8	60.5
		m. s.	m. s.
800 metres		2 34	2 41
1500 metres		5 10	5 28

Girls under 13 years			
		secs.	secs.
80 metres		12.0	13.0
100 metres		14.3	14.6
200 metres		30.8	31.7
Hurdles	70 metres at 68 cm	13.5	14.2
	75 metres at 68 cm	14.5	14.9
Relay	4 × 100 m	60.0	62.2
		m. s.	m. s.
800 metres		2 48	2 57
1500 metres		5 52	6 06

Athletics: Track Events

Boys under 14 years

		D	S
		secs.	secs.
80 metres		11.2	12.0
100 metres		13.0	13.4
200 metres		27.6	28.8
400 metres		62.0	65.0
Hurdles	70 metres at 76 cm	12.6	13.0
	75 metres at 76 cm	13.2	13.9
	80 metres at 76 cm	14.0	15.0
Relay	4 × 100 m	54.7	57.6
		m. s.	m. s.
800 metres		2 27	2 33
1500 metres		4 59	5 19

Girls under 14 years

		D	S
		secs.	secs.
80 metres		11.7	12.2
100 metres		13.9	14.3
200 metres		29.7	30.5
Hurdles	70 metres at 76 cm	13.0	13.8
	75 metres at 76 cm	13.6	14.4
Relay	4 × 100 m	57.8	61.3
		m. s.	m. s.
800 metres		2 44	2 52
1500 metres		5 42	5 56

Boys under 15 years

	D	S
	secs.	secs.
100 metres	12.5	12.7
200 metres	25.8	26.9
400 metres	59.0	61.1
Hurdles	13.2	14.6
Relay	51.2	54.1
	m. s.	m. s.
800 metres	2 19	2 27
1500 metres	4 47	5 05

Girls under 15 years

	D	S
	secs.	secs.
100 metres	13.6	14.1
200 metres	28.5	29.6
Hurdles	13.3	14.1
Relay	56.2	59.8
	m. s.	m. s
800 metres	2 38	2 50
1500 metres	5 30	5 54

Boys under 17 years	D	S
	secs.	secs.
100 metres	12.0	12.1
200 metres	24.8	25.5
400 metres	56.1	58.5
Hurdles (100 m)	15.6	16.4
Hurdles (400 m)	67.0	72.0
Relay	48.7	50.2
	m. s.	m. s.
800 metres	2 10	2 17
1500 metres	4 30	4 49
3000 metres	9 40	10 22
Steeplechase (1500 m)	5 30	5 50

Girls under 17 years		
	secs.	secs.
100 metres	13.4	13.7
200 metres	28.0	29.1
400 metres	66.2	72.3
Hurdles	13.4	14.6
Relay	54.5	58.1
	m. s.	m. s.
800 metres	2 33	2 45
1500 metres	5 25	5 52

(The above tables are reproduced by kind permission of The English Schools Athletic Association from the ESAA *Handbook.* Further information about the ESAA can be obtained from the Hon. Secretary, Mr N. Dickinson, 'Davidiane', 26 Coniscliffe Road, Stanley, Co. Durham, DH9 7RF.)